To:

_____

*This is what the L*ORD *says—*

I have summoned you by name; you are mine.
Isaiah 43:1

From:

_____

Requests for information should be addressed to:
    Inspirio, the gift group of Zondervan
    Grand Rapids, Michigan 49530
    http://www.inspiriogifts.com

Editor: Janice Jacobson
Compiler: Molly C. Detweiler
Design manager: Amy J. Wenger
Project manager: Tom Dean
Art and Design: Koechel Peterson & Associates, Inc., Minneapolis, MN
Printed in China

03 04 05/HK/ 4 3 2

MEDITATIONS *on the* PURPOSE-DRIVEN® LIFE

By RICK WARREN

ψ
inspirio™

"WHY DO I EXIST?"

"WHY AM I HERE?"

"WHAT IS MY PURPOSE?"

THESE ARE THE MOST fundamental questions you can ask in life. Have you ever asked these questions, wondering where to turn for the answers?

The truth is that you were made by God and for God. Until you understand this, life will never make sense. God has never created anything without a purpose. Colossians 1:16 says:

PURPOSE-DRIVEN

For everything, absolutely
everything, above and
below, visible and invisible, . . .
everything got started
in God and finds
its purpose in him" The Message

The very fact that you're alive means God has a purpose for your life!

And you weren't created for just one purpose. You were created for five special reasons that are explained in God's Word, the Bible. This little book will help you understand why you are alive, why you go through difficult circumstances, and what God planned for you to do with your life.

YOU WERE PLANNED for GOD'S PLEASURE!

You, God, . . . created everything

and it is for Your pleasure

that they exist and were created.

Revelation 4:11 NLT

THE BIBLE SAYS THAT GOD IS LOVE.
It doesn't say God *has* love. It says God *is* love.
Love is the essence of his character. God created
you as an object of his love. You were made to be
loved by God—that's your number one purpose.

God didn't *need* to love you. He wasn't lonely.
He didn't need servants. He wasn't bored. God
created humans because he wanted to love us.
We were planned for his pleasure.

The LORD takes pleasure in his people.

Psalm 149:4 NASB

GOD MADE US IN HIS IMAGE.
That means that we are unlike anything else
in all of creation. We alone were given the
capacity to know God and to love him and
to have him know and love us in return.

God created man in his own image,

in the image of God he created him;

male and female he created them.

Genesis 1:27

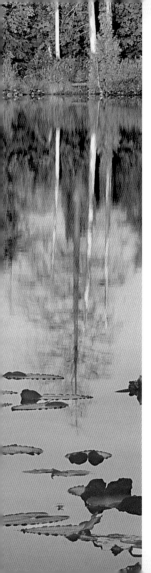

The God who made the world and everything in it is the Lord of heaven and earth. . . . He is not served by human hands, as if he needed anything, because he himself gives all men life and breath and everything else. From one man he made every nation of men, that they should inhabit the whole earth; and he determined the times set for them and the exact places where they should live. God did this so that men would seek him and perhaps reach out for him and find him, though he is not far from each one of us. 'For in him we live and move and have our being.' Acts 17:24–28

THE FIRST PURPOSE FOR YOUR LIFE is to know and to love God because that gives God pleasure.

The most important thing you can know in life is that God loves you.

"I have loved you with an everlasting love;
I have drawn you with loving-kindness," says the Lord.
Jeremiah 31:3

The most important thing you can do in life i love him back.

Love the Lord your God with all your heart
and with all your soul and with all your mind.
This is the first and greatest commandment.
Matthew 22:37–38

God knows everything about you and he still loves you. His deepest desire is for you to know him and love him in return.

"I don't want your sacrifice—
I want your love.
I don't want your offerings—
I want you to know me,"
says the Lord.

Hosea 6:6 LB

Instead of trying to do and say all the right things to make God love you, you need to realize that he already loves you. You just need to learn how to love him back.

God wants to help you to know him and love him more. All you need to do is ask, perhaps with a prayer like this:

God, if I don't get anything else done today, help me to know you a little bit better and love you a little bit more. If, at the end of the day, I know you a little bit better and I love you a little bit more, I will have not wasted this day. On the other hand, it won't matter what else I've done or left undone, if I missed the first purpose of my life. So help me, Father, to know and love you more today.

FULFILLING

PERHAPS YOU'VE BEEN TRYING to find your purpose in life through a career or accomplishments, or a relationship. These things alone, no matter how wonderful and fulfilling, are not your purpose. You were made for far more. You were made to last forever.

It's in Christ that we find out who we are and what we are living for. Long before we first heard of Christ and got our hopes up, he had his eye on us, had designs on us for glorious living, part of the overall purpose he is working out in everything and everyone.   Ephesians. 1:11 *The Message*

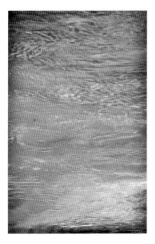

BRINGING ENJOYMENT TO GOD
and living for his pleasure is the first purpose
of your life. When you fully understand this
truth, you'll never again have a problem with
feeling insignificant. It proves your worth.
If God made you to love you, and he values you
enough to keep you with him for eternity, what
greater significance could you have?

The LORD will fulfill his purpose for me;
your love, O LORD, endures forever.
Psalm 138:8

When you love God, you want to express it. That is called *Worship*. Worship
far more than praying or singing in church. You worship when you trust God
mpletely, love him supremely, obey him wholeheartedly, and thank him continu-
ly. Anytime you bring pleasure to God, you are worshipping him! Worship is the
st purpose of your life.

> So then, my friends, because of God's great mercy to us
> I appeal to you: Offer yourselves as a living sacrifice to
> God, dedicated to his service and pleasing to him.
> This is the true worship that you should offer.
>
> Romans 12:1 TEV

Your most profound and intimate experi-
ces of worship will likely be in your darkest
ys—when your heart is broken, when you feel
andoned, when you're out of options, when
e pain is great, and you turn to God alone.
The deepest level of worship is praising God
spite of pain, trusting God during times of
ouble, and loving God when he seems distant.

> The LORD is pleased
> with those who worship
> him and trust his love.
>
> Psalm 147:11 CEV

YOU WERE FORMED
for A FAMILY!

God's unchanging plan has

always been to adopt us into his

own family by bringing us to

himself through Jesus Christ.

And this gave him great pleasure.

Ephesians 1:5 NLT

FROM THE BEGINNING OF TIME, God has always wanted a family. The entire Bible is the story of God building a family who will love him, honor him, and reign with him forever. He wants *you* to be a part of that family—a family that will last for all eternity.

Hebrews 2:11 is an amazing verse:

> *Jesus and the people He makes holy*
> *all belong to the same family.*
> *That's why He isn't ashamed*
> *to call them His brothers and sisters.* NJB

Jesus Christ calls us his brothers and sisters! We're not just called to *believe*. We're called to *belong*—to belong to the family of God.

God has given us the privilege

of being born again so that now

we are members of God's own family.

That family is the church of the living God,

the support and foundation of the truth.

1 Peter 1:3 NJB

WHAT DOES THE FAMILY
OF GOD LOOK LIKE?

WHERE CAN IT BE FOUND?

FOUNDATION

IF A BUILDING HAS NO SUPPORT
and foundation it collapses. In the same way, you
need support from other people and a foundation
to keep you strong in your walk with God. You
find that loving support when you join your
brothers and sisters in Christ's church.

Not only is the church God's family, it is called the body of Christ. When you become part of the family of God, you also become a member of Christ's body. We are all connected and dependent upon each other.

Just as each of us has one body with many members, and these members do not all have the same function, so in Christ we who are many form one body, and each member belongs to all the others.

Romans 12:4–5

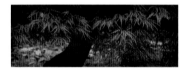

The church is a *body*, not a *business*; a *family* not an *institution*. God said, "I formed you to be a part of my family."

There should be no division in the body, but . . . its parts should have equal concern for each other. If one part suffers, every part suffers with it; if one part is honored, every part rejoices with it. Now you are the body of Christ, and each one of you is a part of it.   1 Corinthians 12:25–27

Whenever you feel discouraged, remember that you are not alone. God has a family to support you and encourage you. Reach out to your brothers and sisters for support.

The more you grow spiritually, the more you're going to love and treasure the church, because Jesus died for the church. Nothing is more valuable to God than his church. He paid the highest price for it, Jesus loves the church so much that the Bible compares it to a beloved bride.

Christ loved the church and gave himself up for her to make her holy, cleansing her by the washing with water through the word, and to present her to himself as a radiant church, without stain or wrinkle or any other blemish, but holy and blameless. Ephesians 5:25–27

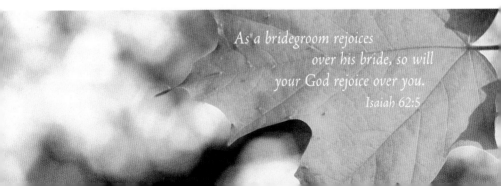

As a bridegroom rejoices over his bride, so will your God rejoice over you. Isaiah 62:5

GOD'S FAMILY

JUST LIKE IN AN EARTHLY FAMILY, where we receive love, but also give it, in God's family we are called to love and care for our fellow members.

There are 58 "one anothers" in the Bible that teach us how to treat our brothers and sisters in the family of God.

They include:

LOVE ONE ANOTHER

Dear friends, since God so loved us, we also ought to love one another. 1 John 4:11

ENCOURAGE ONE ANOTHER

Let us not give up meeting together, as some are in the habit of doing, but let us encourage one another. Hebrews 10:25

❧ SERVE ONE ANOTHER
    Serve one another in love.   Galatians 5:13

❧ PRAY FOR ONE ANOTHER
    Confess your sins to each other
    and pray for each other.   James 5:16

You should be like one big happy family,

full of sympathy toward each other,

loving one another with tender

hearts and humble minds.
1 Peter 3:8 LB

If we walk in the light,

   as God is in the light,

we have fellowship with

   one another, and

the blood of Jesus, his Son,

purifies us from all sin.

     1 John 1:7

WHEN YOU PARTICIPATE in God's family by loving and caring for each other, that's called *Fellowship*. Fellowship is the second purpose of your life.

FELLOWSHIP

Real fellowship means being as committed
to each other as we are to Jesus.
First John 3:16 says:

We understand what real love is when we realize that
Christ gave His life for us. That means that we must
give our lives for other believers. NJB

Giving of yourself and putting others first, isn't
easy, but God asks you do it because he did it
first. He loves us even though we aren't perfect,
and his purpose for you is to do the same. Jesus
wants you to love *real* people, not *ideal* people—
because there are no perfect people.

WHEN WE PLACE OUR FAITH in Christ, God becomes our Father, we become his children, other believers become our brothers and sisters, and the church becomes our spiritual family. The family of God includes all believers in the past, in the present, and all who will believe in the future.

So now you Gentiles are no longer strangers and foreigners. You are citizens along with all of God's holy people. You are members of God's family.
Ephesians 2:19 NLT

Being included in God's family is the highest honor and the greatest privilege you will ever receive. Nothing else comes close. Whenever you feel unimportant, unloved, or insecure, remember who you belong to.

A Christian without a church family is an orphan.

In Christ we who are many form one body, and each member belongs to all the others.
Romans 12:5

Most of all, let love guide your life, for then the whole church will stay together in perfect harmony.
Colossians 3:14 LB

Since God is love, the most important lesson he wants you to learn on earth is how to love. It is in loving that we are most like him, so love is the foundation of every command he's given us: God's whole law can be summed up in this one command: Love others as you love yourself.

God wants us to love everyone, but he is particularly concerned that we learn to love others in his family.

When we have the opportunity to help anyone, we should do it. But we should give special attention to those who are in the family of believers.
Galatians 6:10 NCV

Carry each other's burdens, and in this way you will fulfill the law of Christ.
Galatians 6:2

YOU WERE CREATED to BECOME LIKE CHRIST

From the very beginning God decided

that those who came to Him—

and all along He knew who would—

should become like His Son,

so His Son would be the First with many brothers.

Romans 8:29 LB

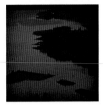

FROM THE VERY BEGINNING,
God's plan has been to make you like his son,
Jesus. This is your destiny and the third
purpose of your life. God announced this
intention at creation:

> Then God said,
>
> "Let us make human beings
>
> in our image and likeness."
>
> Genesis 1:26 NCV

The LORD God formed the man
    from the dust of the ground and breathed
into his nostrils the breath of life,
        and the man became a living being.
            Genesis 2:7

We were made with the very breath of God.

On earth, God's ultimate goal for your life is not comfort but character development! He wants you to grow up spiritually and become like Christ. God is far more interested in what you *are* than in what you *do* because you're not taking your career into heaven, but you are taking your *character*.

> Take on an entirely new way of life—a God-fashioned life, a life renewed from the inside and working itself into your conduct as God accurately reproduces his character in you.
>
> Ephesians 4:22 The Message

It is the Holy Spirit's job to produce Christ-like character in you. The Bible says,

> As the Spirit of the Lord works within us, we become more and more like him and reflect his glory even more.
>
> 2 Corinthians 3:18 LB

IF GOD WANTS TO MAKE US
like Jesus, the question becomes,
"What is Jesus like?"

If you want a perfect picture of Jesus you
can find it in Galatians 5:22–23:

The fruit of the Spirit is love,

joy, peace, patience, kindness,

goodness, faithfulness,

gentleness and self-control.

These nine qualities portray a beautiful
description of Jesus Christ. Jesus is *perfect* love,
joy, peace, patience, and all the other fruit
embodied in a single person. To have the fruit of
the Spirit is to be like Christ.

SO HOW DOES GOD MAKE US LIKE JESUS? Do I just walk down the street one day and . . . zap! I'm full of love! Do I go to a conference or read a book or listen to a tape and . . . bang! I'm filled with patience! No. There's no such thing as instant spiritual maturity.

This next sentence is one of the most important spiritual truths you'll ever learn: God develops Christlike character in you by allowing circumstances where you're tempted to express the exact opposite quality! Character development always involves a choice and temptation provides that opportunity.

It's easy to love lovely people. God teaches you real love by putting you around some unlovely people. It takes no character to love people who are lovely and loving to you.

> Dear children, let us stop just saying we love each other; let us really show it by our actions. 1 John 3:18 NLT

Joy is different than happiness. Happiness depends on external circumstances. Joy is internal, often in spite of circumstances. God will teach you real joy when you turn to him in the middle of grief or depression.

> Dear brothers and sisters, whenever trouble comes your way, let it be an opportunity for joy. For when your faith is tested, your endurance a chance to grow. James 1:2–3 N

PEACE

Where do you learn peace? Out fishing on a beautiful stream? Anybody can be peaceful in that kind of environment. Instead, God will allow days when everything seems to go wrong so you can learn inner peace. It is there, in the middle of the storm, that you learn peace.

> "When you pass through the waters, I will be with you; and when you pass through the rivers, they will not sweep over you. When you walk through the fire, you will not be burned; the flames will not set you ablaze," says the Lord.
>
> Isaiah 43:2

PATIENCE

God's plan for teaching us patience is pretty obvious. He makes us wait. One of the most difficult seasons of life is when we are in a hurry and God isn't. God is never in a hurry and he is never late. God's timing is perfect and he wants you to learn to trust him.

> You know that under pressure, your faith-life is forced into the open and shows its true colors. So don't try to get out of anything prematurely. Let it do its work so you become mature and well-developed, not deficient in any way.
>
> James 1:3–4 The Message

ONCE YOU UNDERSTAND THAT GOD'S
third purpose for your life is to make you like Christ, life
begins to make more sense. When difficult, unexplainable
things happen, we know that God is using it all for this
purpose.

We know that in all things God works for the good of those
who love him, who have been called according to his purpose ...
to be conformed to the likeness of his Son ...
Romans 8:28–29 NIV

As God works in you to make you like his Son, he is
going to take you through the struggles Jesus experienced.

Were there times when Jesus was lonely? — Yes

Were there times when Jesus was tired? — Yes.

Were there times when he was misunderstood and criticized unjustly? — Yes

Did God take care of and strengthen Jesus through it all? — Yes

And he'll do the same for you

In your lives you must think
and act like Jesus Christ.
Philippians 2:5 NCV

Every time you forget that one of God's purposes is to make you like Christ, you'll become frustrated by your circumstances. You'll wonder, "Why is this happening to me? Why am I having such a difficult time?" One answer is that life is supposed to be difficult! As rushing water smooths the rough edges off stones, God is polishing you for eternity.

No matter how difficult the situation, you can grow from it if you will respond to it with the question, "What do you want me to learn, Father?"

THE PROCESS THAT GOD USES to make you like Jesus is called *Discipleship*.

The Bible says "*. . . we arrive at real maturity— that measure of development which is meant by 'the fullness of Christ.'*" Christlikeness is the destination you'll eventually arrive at, but your journey will last a lifetime.

We will be mature just like Christ is and we will be completely like Him.
Ephesians 4:13 NJB

Speaking the truth in love,

we will in all things grow up into him

who is the Head, that is, Christ.
Ephesians 4:15

Today, we're obsessed with speed but God is more interested in strength and stability, than swiftness. We want the quick fix, the shortcut. But real maturity takes time. Growth is gradual. The Bible says,

Our lives gradually becoming brighter and more beautiful as God enters our lives and we become like him.
2 Corinthians 3:18 The Message

God is not in a hurry to make you like Jesus. In fact, he will take your entire lifetime to mold you. We get in a hurry but he isn't in a hurry.

Often we get discouraged and think, "I'm not growing. I'm not maturing fast enough." But God has promised to never give up on us.

God who began

a good work in us

will bring it to the

day of completion.
Philippians 1:6 NJB

WHY DOES IT TAKE SO LONG to change, get well, and grow up? There are several reasons: We forget what we learn and have to learn it again; We have to unlearn many wrong ideas; We are afraid to honestly face the truth about ourselves; Growth can be painful and scary; It takes time to develop godly habits.

These things I plan won't happen

right away. Slowly, steadily,

surely, the time approaches when

the vision will be fulfilled. If it

seems slow, do not despair, for

these things will surely come to

pass. Just be patient! They will

not be overdue a single day!

Habbakuk 2:3 LB

Don't get discouraged and don't give up! Remember how far you've come, not just how far you have to go. You are not where you want to be, but neither are you where you used to be. Your heavenly Father is not waiting for you to be perfect or even mature before he loves you. He loves you at evey stage of growth.

YOU WERE SHAPED
for SERVING GOD!

God has made us what we are. And in Christ Jesus,

God has made us to do good works which

God planned in advance for us to live our lives doin.

Ephesians 2:10 NCV

*T*HE BIBLE SAYS you are uniquely shaped.

You shaped me first inside and then out.

You formed me in my mother's womb.

Psalm 139:13 *The Message*

S —SPIRITUAL GIFTS: Special gifts given by the
Holy Spirit to help others in God's family.

H —HEART: Special passions, things that you feel
strongly about, to use for God's glory.

A —ABILITIES: Natural talents built into you
from birth.

P —PERSONALITY: Your uniqueness, what makes
you different from every one else.

E —EXPERIENCES: Situations and circumstances
you face that help you empathize with others.

God custom-made you with these five factors
to prepare you to serve him.

Before I made you
in your mother's
womb, I chose you.
Before you were
born, I set you
apart for a special
work.
Jeremiah 1:5 NCV

YOU WEREN'T PLACED ON EARTH
just to breathe, eat, take up space, and have fun.
God fashioned and formed you to make a unique
contribution with your life. You were put here to
give something back, not just get; to add to life on
earth, not just take from it. God designed you to
make a difference. Service to God and others is
the fourth purpose for your life.

You're not saved by service but you are saved
for service. In God's Kingdom, you have a place,
a purpose, a role, and a function to fulfill. This
gives your life great significance and value.

It is he who saved us and chose us for

his holy work not because we deserved it but

because that was his plan . . . .
        2 Timothy 1:9 LB

EXPERIENCES are one of the most important things that God uses to shape you for service. There are five kinds of experiences God uses:

- Family experiences—interactions with parents, children, spouses, and anyone you call family.
- Vocational experiences—everything you learn on the job, from skills to getting along with others.
- Educational experiences—times of learning throughout your life, from elementary school to continuing discovery as an adult.
- Spiritual experiences—those special moments of incredible closeness with God, when you discover something new about who he is and who you are in him.

But most important of all:

- Painful experiences—disappointments, hurts, and sorrows cause you to lean heavily on God, and develop empathy in your heart for the hurts of others.

Painful experiences are hard to understand.
We ask God, "Why me?"

But . . .

- 🍃 Who can better help the parents of a handicapped child than other parents of a handicapped child?
- 🍃 Who can better help somebody going through the pain of divorce than somebody else who has gone through one?
- 🍃 Who can better help an alcoholic than somebody who has also struggled with alcoholism?

Often, the very problem that you struggle most with in life, the very thing you like the least about yourself or your circumstances, the very experience that you're most embarrassed and ashamed of, is the tool God wants to use in you to bless, encourage, and minister to others. God uses not just our strengths. He also uses our weaknesses.

Jesus said, "My grace is sufficient for you, for my power is made perfect in weakness." Therefore I will boast all the more gladly about my weaknesses, so that Christ's power may rest on me.
2 Corinthians 12:9

We are only fully alive when we're helping others.

Jesus said,

"If you insist on saving your life, you will lose it.
Only those who throw away their lives for my sake
and for the sake of the Good News will ever know
what it means to really live."

Mark 8:35 LB

WHY DOES GOD use our weaknesses? Because when he does, he gets all the glory. If God only used your strengths, others would look at you and either be jealous (Why didn't I get that talent?) or discouraged (I'll never be like that!). But when God uses you in spite of your weaknesses, it gives people hope. They realize "God could use me too!"

Your weaknesses are not an accident. God deliberately allowed them in your life for the purpose of demonstrating his power through you.

Paul wrote,

for Christ's sake, I delight in weaknesses,

in insults, in hardships, in persecutions,

in difficulties. For when I am weak,

then I am strong.

2 Corinthians 12:10

GOD HAS GIVEN YOU A UNIQUE S.H.A.P.E. There is no one else in the world just like you. Only you can be you! Using your spiritual gifts, heart, abilities, personality, and experiences for the benefit of others is called your *Ministry*. Ministry, or service, is the fourth purpose of your life.

God has given each of you some special abilities.
Be sure to use them to help each other,
passing on to others God's many kinds of blessing.
1 Corinthians 12:7 NJB

You have dozens of hidden abilities and gifts that you don't know you've got because you've never tried them out. I encourage you to try doing some things you've never done before. Until you're actually involved in serving, you're not going to know what you're good at.

Since we find ourselves fashioned into all these excellently formed
and marvelously functioning parts in Christ's body,
let's just go ahead and be what we were made to be.
Romans 12:5 The Message

Satan will try to steal the joy of service from you by tempting you to compare your ministry to others, and by tempting you to conform your ministry to the expectations of others. Both are deadly traps that will distract you from serving in the ways God intended for you to serve

The Bible warns us to never compare ourselves with others:

Do your own work well, and then you will have something to be proud of.
But don't compare yourself with others.
Galatians 6:4 CEV

Using your God-given shape in ministry is the secret of fruitfulness and fulfillment. God wants you to be you! The better your area of service fits your shape, the more successful you'll be.

YOU WERE MADE
for A MISSION!

Jesus prayed to his Father,

*In the same way that You gave
Me a mission in the world,
I give them a mission in the world.*
John 17:18 The Message

GOD HAS A MISSION FOR YOU in the world.

*Through Christ God has made peace between us and Himself
and He gave us the work of telling everyone the peace we can
have with Him. So we have been sent to speak for Christ.*
2 Corinthians 5:19–20 NJB

If you want God's blessing and power on your life, you must care about what God cares about most. The biggest concern of God's heart is bringing his lost children back home to him.

*The most important thing is that I complete my mission,
the work that the Lord Jesus gave me, to tell people
the good news about His grace.*
Acts 20:24 NCV

Our mission on earth is to be ambassadors for God! God loves people so much that he has sent us to represent him to those who don't yet know him. This is your mission to the world.

God created you to have a *ministry* in the church and a *mission* in the world. Both are important! Fulfilling your mission in the world is called *Evangelism*. It is—the fifth purpose of your life.

Once you become part of God's family it's your mission to tell others the Good News about Jesus and God's five purposes for our lives.

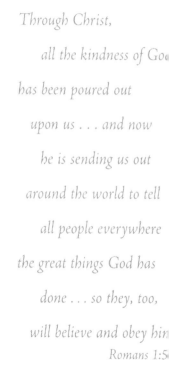

Through Christ,

all the kindness of God

has been poured out

upon us . . . and now

he is sending us out

around the world to tell

all people everywhere

the great things God has

done . . . so they, too,

will believe and obey him

Romans 1:5

ETERNAL LIFE

The Lord is not slow in keeping his promise,

   as some understand slowness.

He is patient with you,

    not wanting anyone to perish,

      but everyone to come to repentance.

2 Peter 3:9

God so loved the world
that he gave his one and
only Son, that whoever
believes in him shall not
perish but have eternal life.

John 3:16

MY FATHER WAS a minister for over fifty years, serving mostly in small, rural churches. He was a simple preacher, but he was a man with a mission. His favorite activity was taking teams of volunteers overseas to build church buildings for small congregations. In his lifetime, dad built over 150 churches around the world.

In 1999, my dad contracted cancer. In the final week of his life, the disease kept him awake in a semi-conscious state nearly 24 hours a day. As he dreamed, he'd talk out loud what he was dreaming. Sitting by his bedside, I learned a lot about my dad, just listening to his dreams. He relived one church building project after another.

One night near the end, while my wife, niece, and I were by his side, dad suddenly became very active and tried to get out of bed. Of course he was too weak, and my wife insisted he lie back down. But he persisted in trying to get out of bed, so my wife finally asked, "Jimmy, what are you trying to do?" He replied, "Got to save one more for Jesus! Got to save one more for Jesus! Got to save one more for Jesus!" He began to repeat that phrase over and over.

During the next hour, he said it probably a hundred times. "Got to save one more for Jesus!" As I sat by his bed with tears flowing down my cheeks, I bowed my head to thank God for my dad's faith. At that moment, he reached out and placed his frail hand on my head and said as commissioning me, "Save one more for Jesus! Save one more for Jesus!" I intend for that to be the theme of the rest of my life. I invite you to consider it as a focus for your life too, because nothing else will make a greater difference for eternity. God wants his lost children found! Nothing matters more to God; the Cross proves that. I pray that you will always be on the lookout to reach *one more for Jesus* so when you stand before God one day, you can say "Mission accomplished!"

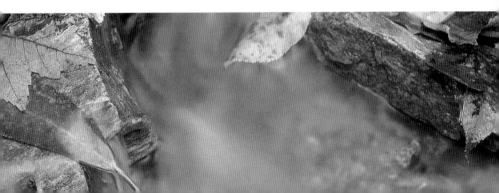

The fruit of the righteous

is a tree of life

and he who wins souls is wise.
Proverbs 11:30

Those who believe in the

Son of God have the testimony

of God in them."

1 John 5:10
God's Word Translation

God has put a life message within you.
Your life Message has four parts to it:

Your *testimony:* the story of how you began
relationship with Jesus.

Your *life lessons:* the most important lessons
God has taught you.

Your *godly passions:* the issues God shaped you
care about most.

The *Good News:* the message of salvation.

YOU WERE MADE TO LIVE

a purpose-driven life!

God's five purposes of your life are:

1. WORSHIP: You were planned for God's pleasure!

After all this, there is only one thing to say:
Have reverence for God, and obey his commands,
because this is all that we were created for.

Ecclesiastes 12:13 TEV

2. FELLOWSHIP: You were formed for a family

It was a happy day for him when he gave us our new lives
through the truth of his Word, and we became, as it were,
the first children in his new family.

James 1:18 LB

3. DISCIPLESHIP: You were created to become like Christ!

God knew what he was doing from the very beginning.
He decided from the outset to shape the lives of those
who love him along the same lines as the life of his Son
We see the original and intended shape of our lives there in

Romans 8:29 The Message

4. MINISTRY: You were shaped for serving God!

For we are God's workmanship,
created in Christ Jesus to do good works,
which God prepared in advance for us to do.
Ephesians 2:10

5. EVANGELISM: You were made for a mission.

Jesus said, "Go and make disciples of all
nations, baptizing them in the name
of the Father and of the Son
and of the Holy Spirit, and teaching
them to obey everything I have commanded you.
And surely I am with you always,
to the very end of the age."
Matthew 28:19–20

Many years ago, I noticed a little phrase in Acts 13:36 that forever altered the direction of my life:

David ... served the purpose of God in his own generation ...
Acts 13:36 NASB

Now I understood why God called David *"a man after my own heart."* He dedicated his life to fulfilling God's purposes on earth. There is n greater epitaph than that statement! Imagine it chiseled on your tombstone: You served God's purpose in your generation! It's my prayer that people will be able to say that about you. That's why I wrote this book for you.

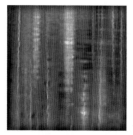

Regardless of your age the rest of your life car be the best of your life if you start living on pur pose today.

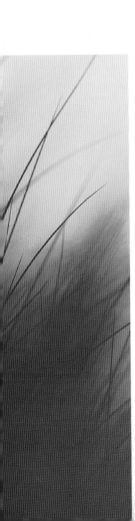

A LIFE-CHANGING PRAYER

Father, more than anything else I want to live for you and the five purposes that you created me to fulfill.

I want my life to bring you pleasure as I live a lifestyle of worship.

I want to be used to build the fellowship of your family, the church.

I want to become like Jesus in the way I think and feel and act.

I want to use the shape you've given me for a ministry to other believers in the Body of Christ.

I want to fulfill my mission in the world by telling others about your love. Help me to reach one more for Jesus. Help me to pass on the message of your purposes to others.

Dear Lord, I want to serve your purposes in my generation so that one day I may hear you say, "Well done, good and faithful servant."

In Jesus' name, Amen.

SOURCES